Kalmus Chamber I

PERCY ALDRIDGE
GRAINGER

HILL SONG No. 1

1921 version

FULL SCORE

EDWIN F. KALMUS, CO.

INSTRUMENTATION

Piccolo
Flute
Oboe
English Horn
Bassoon
Double Bassoon

Sopranino Sarrusophone in E flat
(Alt. Oboe II)
Tenor Sarrusophone in B flat
(Alt. Bass Oboe [hecklphone],
Tenor Saxophone, or Bass Clarinet)
Soprano Saxophone in B flat
(Alt. Clarinet in B flat)
Alto Saxophone in E flat
(Alt. Alto Clarinet or Horn in E flat)

Horn in F
Trumpet in B flat
Euphonium

Percussion (1 player)
Timpani and Cymbals

Harmonium
Piano

Strings
(1.1.2.2.1)

Duration: approx. 15 minutes

PUBLISHER PROGRAM NOTE

Hill Song No. 1 is one of the most audacious and forward-looking of all the works by Percy Grainger. Begun in March 1901 while he was still a student at the Höch Conservatoire in Frankfurt, it is one of Grainger's earliest surviving compositions, though Grainger recalled it was a distillation of a number of techniques he tried out experimentally in the late 1890s; "wide-tone scales," "irregular rhythms," "democratic polyphony," and "semi-discordant triads" among them. A passage toward the end that bears a misty resemblance to impressionist harmony was inspired, as Grainger admits, by seeing part of the score of Debussy's Pelleas et Mélisande in 1902. The first version of Hill Song No. 1 was completed in London in September 1902. The most radical thing about Hill Song No. 1 was its scoring, and indeed, this is what kept it out of the ears of the public for decades. It is scored for 24 winds -- two piccolos, six oboes, six English horns, six bassoons, and contra-bassoon. Due to his relative inexperience as a composer and German training -- after all, he was only 19 years old when he wrote the work -- Grainger spelled out compound rhythms in archaic ways, such as identifying a bar of 5/8 as "two and a half over four." Such rhythmic divisions are scattered throughout all of the 24 parts, with some differing divisions laid on top of one another; the best wind players in the world in 1902 could not read or play the Hill Song No. 1, which is what Grainger realized once he tried to mount a performance of the work. In 1907, he created the short, pithy Hill Song No. 2, which places some of the elements of the earlier piece in a more conventional context and is less than a third as long as the original. In 1921, he completely rebarred and rescored the Hill Song No. 1 for an ensemble of piccolo, flute, six double reeds, two saxophones, three brass, harmonium, percussion, piano, and six string parts. The added instruments were designed to address Grainger's concern about wheeziness of the high number of double reeds in the original version; he also created a version for two pianos at the same time.

-Uncle Dave Lewis, AllMusic.com (excerpt)

HILL-SONG Nr. I.

Program-note.

My Hill-Songs arose out of thoughts about and longings for the wildness of hill countries, hill peoples and hill musics (such as the Scottish Highlands, the Himalayas, the bagpipes, and the like).

Hill-song Nr. I was composed in 1901 and 1902,* and was scored in 1902** for 21 wood-wind instruments (2 small flutes, 6 oboes, 6 English horns, 6 bassoons, 1 double-bassoon).

This original scoring not being feasible it was rescored in 1921 (June—December) for the present combination of instruments, certain further minor revisions of scoring being undertaken in 1923 (March—May).

PERCY ALDRIDGE GRAINGER.

* The musical material of Hill-song Nr. I was composed as follows:
Bars 1—9, 383—397 (and maybe some others of a kindred type) date from March 16, 1901, and thenabouts, in Frankfurt-am-Main, Germany. Most of the fast elements, such as bars 286—382, date from the later half of the summer of 1902, at Waddesdon, Buckinghamshire, England.

All the rest dates from (and including) the summer of 1901 to (and including) the earlier half of the summer of 1902, in Kensington, London.

** Toward the end of the summer (up to September 1 st), at Waddesdon, Buckinghamshire, England.

To the conductor.

All the parts are concieved as strictly Single parts, and the string parts must not be doubled or massed, even if the work is given in a large hall.

Passages within the brackets ⌐ ¬ are to be played to the fore, as solos. (The signs ⌐ ¬ are adapted from a score by Arnold Schönberg.) Passages marked "accomp" are to be played accompanyingly (quasi accompagnamento).

Thruout the "2 nd speed" (that begins with bar 46) the waywardness of time should show a general leaning towards quickening while loudening, towards slackening while softening. During "2 nd speed" also linger somewhat on the climaxes (top notes) of phrases.

In the harmonium part ⑧ indicates 8 foot stops, ⑯ indicates 16 foot stops, ④ indicates 4 foot stops. (Full) indicates "Full organ".
With regard to pitch the harmonium part is always written as it should be played—not always at actual pitch. Thus all passages marked ⑯ appear an octave higher than the actual sound intended. The harmonium should provide a rich and ample harmonic background for the 12 (or 13) wind instruments. If you

BERGLIED Nr. I.

Programm-Notiz.

Meine Berglieder sind entsprungen aus Sehnsucht nach der Wildheit der Landschaften, der Bewohner und der Musik der Berge und aus Gedanken darüber. Unter anderem schwebten mir vor das schottische Hochland, die Himalajas, schottisches und asiatisches Dudelsackspiel.

Berglied Nr. I wurde in den Jahren 1901—1902* komponiert, und 1902** für 21 Holzbläser (2 kleine Flöten, 6 Oboen, 6 Englische Hörner, 6 Fagotte, 1 Kontrafagott) instrumentiert. Da diese Instrumentation mich nicit befriedigte, wurde das Werk im Jahre 1921 für die jetzige Besetzung uminstrumentiert, wozu 1923 noch einige weitere kleine Änderungen der Instrumentation vorgenommen wurden.

PERCY ALDRIDGE GRAINGER.

* Der musikalische Stoff zum „Berglied Nr. I" entstand zu verschiedenen Zeitpunkten: Takt 1—9, 383—397 (auch einige andere verwandte Stellen) datieren aus der Zeit um den 16. März 1901 und entstanden in Frankfurt am Main. Das Material zu den bewegteren Teilen (wie zum Beispiel Takt 286—382 ist zum Großteil in der zweiten Hälfte des Sommers 1902 in Waddesdon, Buckinghamshire (England) entstanden.

Das übrige datiert aus dem Sommer 1901 und der Zeit bis zur ersten Hälfte des Sommers 1902 (inklusive) in Kensington, London.

** In Waddesdon, Buckinghamshire (England), vom Spätsommer bis zum 1. September.

An den Dirigenten.

Alle Stimmen sind durchaus als Solostimmen gedacht und selbst wenn das Werk in großen Sälen aufgeführt werden sollte, dürfen die Streicherstimmen nicht verdoppelt oder mehrfach besetzt werden.

Zwischen den Klammern ⌐ ¬ befindliche Phrasen sind hervortretend, solistisch zu spielen. (Die Zeichen ⌐ ¬ sind einer Arnold Schönbergschen Partitur entlehnt und hier etwas umgestaltet.) Die mit „accomp" bezeichneten Stellen sind begleitend, zurücktretend zu spielen.

Im Andante rubato (bei Takt 46 eintretendes Tempo II), wo immer es sich findet, soll das Rubato hauptsächlich darin bestehen, daß sich zum Crescendo etwas Accelerando, zum Decrescendo etwas Ritardando gesellt. Ferner ist beim Andante rubato häufig ein Verweilen auf den Höhepunkten der melodischen Phrasen beabsichtigt.

In der Harmoniumstimme sind Register von 8 Fuß mit ⑧ Register von 16 Fuß mit ⑯, Register von 4 Fuß mit ④ bezeichnet. „Volles Werk" ist mit (Full) angegeben.
In Bezug auf die Oktavenhöhe ist die Harmoniumstimme immer so geschrieben wie sie zu spielen ist — aber nicht immer dem wirklichem Klang entsprechend. So stehen z. B .alle Stellen, die mit ⑯ bezeichnet sind, eine Oktave höher als der beabsichtigte wirkliche Klang.

cannot get a single harmonium powerful enough use 2 or 3 harmoniums, doubling or trebling on the harmonium part.

———————

All the double-reeds (oboes, English horn, bassoon, double-bassoon, sarrusophones) should be played with a very stiff reed, so as to produce a wild, nasal, "bagpipe" quality of tone. The gentle emasculated tone-quality produced by a soft reed (as normally used by most players) is utterly out of place in this composition. The saxophones should produce as reedy a tone as possible.

Do not try to subdue the naturally robuster saxophone and sarrusophone tone down to the volume of a clarinet or an oboe; the office of the saxophones and sarrusophones is to provide a tonal strength midway between the volume of the woodwind and the volume of the brass.

All the reed instruments should play with plenty of vibrato, particularly in the espressivo passages.

———————

In the case of the more unusual time-signatures a down-beat is intended after each dotted barline, tho not so marked a down-beat (nct from so great a height) as at the beginning of such bars. The following methods of beating time are recommended:

Das Harmonium soll den 12 (oder 13) Blasinstrumenten einen vollen, ausreichenden, harmonischen Hintergrund bieten. Sollte kein einzelnes Harmonium aufzutreiben sein, dessen Tonfülle hierzu genügt, so kann die Harmonium stimme zweifach oder dreifach auf 2 oder 3 Harmoniums gespielt werden.

———————

Alle Doppelrohrblatt-Instrumente (Oboen, Englisch Horn, Fagott, Kontrafagott, Sarrusophone) sollen mit sehr hartem Blatt gespielt werden, so daß ein herber, nasaler, schalmeiartiger Ton erzeugt wird. Der zarte entmännlichte Ton eines weichen Blattes (wie es von den meisten Bläsern gebraucht wird), wäre in dieser Komposition gänzlich verfehlt. Auch die Saxophone sollen einen äußerst schalmeiartigen Ton hervorbringen.

Der von Natur robustere Ton der Saxophone und Sarrusophone soll nicht auf die Tonstärke einer Klarinette oder einer Oboe abgedämpft werden; vielmehr sollen die Saxophone und Sarrusophone eine zwischen den Stärkegraden der Holz- und Blechinstrumente liegende Stufe der Tonstärke bilden.

Bei allen Rohrblattinstrumenten ist bei Espressivo-Phrasen recht viel Vibrato gedacht.

———————

Bei den ungewöhnlicheren Taktvorzeichnungen ist immer nach jedem punktierten Taktstrich ein Herunterschlag des Taktstocks gedacht, jedoch sollen diese Bewegungen kleiner sein (aus einer geringeren Höhe) als am Anfang des Taktes. Die folgenden Dirigiermethoden sind zu empfehlen:

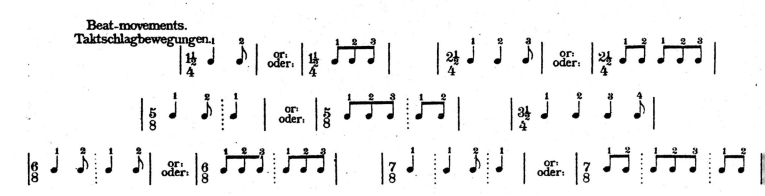

HILL-SONG (Nʀ I)
for room-music 22-some (23-some at will)
by
PERCY ALDRIDGE GRAINGER

composed 1901-1902
rescored June-Dec, 1921
scoring revised March-May, 1923

EDWIN F. KALMUS & CO., INC.

15

26

168

249
255

44

48

368

Les cahiers d'exercices ASSiMiL®

Anglais

LV1 Collège 3e LV1

Hélène Bauchart

À propos de ce cahier

Le cahier que tu t'apprêtes à découvrir est divisé en 3 parties : une consacrée à la grammaire, une à la prononciation, dans laquelle tu apprendras quelques règles à connaître pour partir du bon pied, et une à la culture et à la civilisation, dans laquelle tu découvriras quelques aspects des pays anglophones. La méthode du cahier repose sur une construction progressive des connaissances, que tu pourras assimiler de manière rapide et motivante tout en t'amusant. Au fil des pages, elle te permettra d'apprendre à échanger efficacement en anglais. Nous te conseillons de faire les sections et les unités dans l'ordre où elles apparaissent. Pourquoi ? Parce que tu auras besoin d'avoir acquis les connaissances grammaticales de chaque unité pour passer à la suivante, puis pour effectuer la partie « Culture et civilisation », qui est conçue de manière à réactiver tes nouvelles compétences dans un contexte plus large. Dans cette partie, les mots de vocabulaire déjà croisés, très transparents, déductibles en contexte ou à partir de ce que tu connais n'ont pas été traduits, pour solliciter ta réflexion. Il est en effet important que tu apprennes à construire ou déduire du sens à partir des connaissances dont tu disposes.

Pour la prononciation, le tableau des sons fourni sur le rabat de la couverture te donnera quelques repères pour démarrer dans l'apprentissage. Tu verras que les sons sont donnés entre crochets. Ils correspondent à des sonorités françaises proches des sons anglais.

D'un point de vue pratique, ce cahier permet de t'autoévaluer à plusieurs niveaux : après chaque exercice, dessine l'expression de tes icônes : ☺ pour une majorité de bonnes réponses, 😐 pour environ la moitié et ☹ pour moins de la moitié. À la fin de chaque unité, reporte le nombre d'icônes de ces exercices et, en fin d'ouvrage, fais le bilan en reportant les icônes des fins d'unités dans le tableau général fourni.

Allez, à toi de jouer maintenant ! C'est parti !

Sommaire